100

THINGS TO DO ON
MACKINAC
ISLAND
BEFORE YOU
DIE

100
THINGS TO DO ON
MACKINAC ISLAND
BEFORE YOU
DIE

• •

KATH USITALO

REEDY PRESS

Library of Congress Control Number: 2017957322

ISBN: 9781681061290

Design by Jill Halpin

Printed in the United States of America
18 19 20 21 22   5 4 3 2 1

All photos by Kath Usitalo.

Also by Kath Usitalo for Reedy Press: *100 Things to Do in the Upper Peninsula Before You Die* (2017).

Please note that websites, phone numbers, addresses, and company names are subject to change or cancellation. We did our best to relay the most accurate information available, but due to circumstances beyond our control, please do not hold us liable for misinformation. When exploring new destinations, please do your homework before you go.

DEDICATION

To Dixie Franklin, whose writing I've always admired, and who has been an inspiration and travel-writing guru throughout my freelance career. And to my daughter, Paige, who would wear home certain Grand Hotel upholstery fabric if she could.

● ●

CONTENTS

• •

Music and Entertainment

Sports and Recreation

• •

• •

Shopping and Fashion

• •

PREFACE

At 3.8 square miles, Mackinac Island occupies a small piece of the planet, but a huge place in the hearts of those who've embraced its natural beauty, multicultural history, and authentic (albeit largely sanitized) Victorian charms. Located in the Straits of Mackinac, between Michigan's upper and lower peninsulas, its fabric is woven of Native American, French, British, and American purpose, claims, influence, stories, and people. A spiritual home for the Anishnaabek (Odawa, Ojibwa, and Potawatomi), it evolved into an important center for the fur trade and commercial fishing, and a contested military outpost. Since the late 1800s, Mackinac Island has grown into its role as a tourist destination that too many people perceive as worthy of—or only affordable as—a day trip. If that.

Growing up in the Detroit area with four siblings, I made annual trips with my family to visit relatives in the Upper Peninsula. As we crossed the Mackinac Bridge, the five-mile link between the Lower Peninsula and the UP, we'd see the ferries shuttling passengers (no cars) to that island to the east. I wondered about the long, gleaming white building that was visible from miles away. Our family of seven never dreamed of staying at what Mom would call the "hoity-toity" Grand Hotel. It wasn't until I worked in Michigan's tourism industry that I came to appreciate Mackinac Island and the people and passions that preserve and care for its treasures, while striving to create an experience approachable for just about anyone who makes the effort to reach it.

• •

And it does take some planning to get there. Surrounded by the waters of lakes Huron and Michigan, it is accessible only by water or air. Motor vehicles were banned in 1898 (see note below). Mackinac Island belongs to the Upper Peninsula but is a world away from the sprawling wilderness of the UP, which is home to about 306,000 Yoopers (UP-ers). More than three times that number visit Mackinac Island in its six-month tourism season, and most of those one million are day-trippers, who have enough time to see only a fraction of the sights before catching the ferry back to the mainland.

There's no shortage of travel media and industry accolades to support a visit to Mackinac Island. With this book, I enumerate many of those reasons, and I hope to encourage you to make a day trip if that's all you have. But please consider the reasons and ways to spend more time, whether it's one night or several.

Things to keep in mind when planning a visit to Mackinac Island:

- This is a year-round community of about five hundred residents, and although just a few businesses are open in winter, visitors are welcome year-round.
- Prime tourism season is May through October, and in summer Mackinac Island receives up to fifteen thousand visitors daily.
- When the last ferry of the day departs, you feel as though you have the island to yourself.

• •

- Fall is lovely, quiet, and pretty with the changing foliage, and my favorite time to visit.
- Cell and Wi-Fi service can be spotty, but you will survive.
- Exceptions to the ban on motor vehicles for personal use are made for individuals with proof of medical necessity who rely on motorized transport.
- The natural landscape and historical nature of the island's attractions and lodging may present challenges for people with mobility issues; consult the Mackinac Island Tourism Bureau website and individual attractions and businesses for details, planning, and assistance.
- Zip code for all of Mackinac Island is 49757
- For visitor information:
  - o Mackinac Island Tourism Bureau: mackinacisland.org
  - o Upper Peninsula Travel and Recreation Association: uptravel.com
  - o Pure Michigan: michigan.org

In the Yooper tradition I extend the greeting, Welcome to da UP, eh!

—Kath

• •

ACKNOWLEDGMENTS

I appreciate the suggestions from all those folks who, at signings for my book *100 Things to Do in the Upper Peninsula Before You Die*, were excited to share what they love about Mackinac Island, and what draws them back to this special spot in the Great Lakes.

Many thanks to my friends and associates in the Mackinac Island, Upper Peninsula, and Pure Michigan tourism communities for your ideas, assistance, and encouragement. I owe you a Double Fudge Martini. One for each of you—I won't make you share.

• •

FOOD AND DRINK

SIP A BREW WITH A VIEW
AT THE FORT MACKINAC TEA ROOM

After touring the island's 1780 military outpost, you may think that you wouldn't want to live under the spare conditions of the day—that is, until you stop at the original Officers' Stone Quarters. The building now houses the Fort Mackinac Tea Room, a quaint name for a casual indoor/outdoor café. As you soak in the stunning view from your patio table 150 feet above the straits, cold beverage in hand, your tomato basil bisque arrives. Forgetting that a typical army diet was built on beans, bread, and bacon, you reconsider your impression of a Mackinac soldier's lot in life. And you decide it's time for a Grand Hotel pecan ice cream ball with chocolate sauce.

7127 Huron Rd., 906-847-6327
grandhotel.com

CHOW DOWN
AT CHUCKWAGON

In a sliver of a Main Street storefront, the Chuckwagon's griddle sizzles as it has since the 1950s, with locals and tourists seated elbow to elbow at the counter just feet from the short-order action. Each morning 'til eleven, the cook orchestrates a nonstop stream of hash browns, bacon, eggs, and the scrambled stuffing for the popular breakfast burrito. After that, it's time to grill onions for the Mackinac cheese steak, deep-fry piles of fries, and flip a variety of one-third-pound beef patties. Don't miss the diner's soon-to-be-famous bleu cheese burger, topped with a secret sauce. Kitschy cowboy art, the friendly staff, cozy quarters, fair prices, and good cookin' explain the lines outside the door for breakfast and lunch daily.

7400 Main St., 906-847-0019
chuckwagononmackinac.com

PERK UP
AT LUCKY BEAN

Lucky Bean Coffeehouse isn't just another java joint. You may think you're dropping in for an espresso, latte, or plain cuppa joe, but, like legions of LB lovers, you'll likely become a fan who returns for the inviting vibe, engaging crew, and, of course, the well-crafted beverages. The special house brew, Love Potion #9, tops the menu of coffee drinks, smoothies, frappés, chai tea, and baked goods at Carolyn May's café (her family has a long and sweet Mackinac connection through May's fudge). Kick back indoors with the tempting aromas and convivial atmosphere—and, reportedly, the fastest Wi-Fi on the island—or grab a sidewalk table and take in the passing parade of people, horses, and bicyclists. Be sure to bag some beans for brewing Mackinac memories back home.

7383 Market St., 248-342-2988
facebook.com/luckybeancoffee

HAVE YACHTS OF FUN
AT THIS HOT (PINK) SPOT

Unless you suffer from rhodophobia—the fear of the color pink—the Chippewa Hotel's legendary waterfront spot, named by *Thrillist* as the most iconic bar in Michigan, is a must. The Pink Pony has been pouring adult beverages since 1948 and is a favorite watering hole of sailors who are promised "yachts and yachts of fun." As musicians take the stage, backed by a mural of a high-kicking, horsey chorus line, the lively crowd downs specialty drinks, such as the tropical Rum Runner topped with a Captain Morgan's pineapple floater, or one of twenty Michigan beers on tap. You can also opt to sip plain pink lemonade from the signature glass with the strutting pony logo—which is pink, of course.

7221 Main St., 800-241-3341 or 906-847-3341
pinkponymackinac.com

TIP
The Pink Pony serves breakfast, lunch, dinner, and a kids' menu in a dining room with views of the harbor and outdoors under hot pink patio umbrellas, smack dab on the water.

PAUSE FOR A TREAT
AT SADIE'S ICE CREAM PARLOR

When your name is Sadie (officially GCH Roundtown Mercedes of Maryscot), you win "Best in Show" at the 2010 Westminster Kennel Club Dog Show, and your owners hold the keys to an iconic Mackinac resort, you may get a very special retirement present. Amelia and R. D. Musser put the cherry on top of their black Scottish terrier's career by immortalizing their champ with Sadie's Ice Cream Parlor at Grand Hotel. At Sadie's, Scottie-shaped chocolates top bowls of Michigan's delicious Hudsonville Ice Cream, and the eight-scoop Grand Sundae is served in a dog bone-shaped dish. You don't have to be a hotel guest to step inside designer Carleton Varney's fanciful interpretation of an old-fashioned ice cream emporium to have a scoop. Or three, in honor of Sadie's dog show Triple Crown.

1891 Cadotte Ave., 906-847-3331
grandhotel.com

TIP

Good Day Café on Main Street
scoops nationally famous Moomers
Homemade Ice Cream, made by a family
in Traverse City, Michigan.

7216 Main St.
gooddaycafemackinac.com

BITE 'EM LIKE YA MEAN IT
AT CANNONBALL DRIVE INN

About halfway around the island, give or take a mile, you'll see a cannon on the beach at British Landing, the spot where British soldiers landed in July 1812 to attack the Americans and capture Fort Mackinac. It's also the home of Cannonball Drive Inn, named for the stray ammunition that washed up on the shore after the War of 1812. The old-style, walk-up snack shack and ice cream stand is known for rave-worthy deep-fried pickles that come with the command, "Bite 'em like ya mean it!" The Cannonball dates only to 1905, but as you munch your snack while gazing across the water, ponder how the course of history would have changed had it been there about a century earlier to distract the Brits with those deep-fried pickles.

7641 British Landing Rd., 906-847-0932
facebook.com/cannonball.inn

GO NUTS
FOR A GRAND HOTEL TRADITION

Since it debuted in 1947, the Grand Pecan Ball has become the signature dessert of Grand Hotel and is served more than sixty thousand times in the resort's six-month season. Deceptively simple, the secret is the quality of ingredients: a scoop of Michigan's own Hudsonville vanilla ice cream, coated in toasted pecan pieces and set in a puddle of chocolate fudge sauce that is made fresh daily in the Grand Hotel kitchen. You can indulge at the resort's main dining room, as well as Grand Hotel's Jockey Club, Woods Restaurant, the Gate House, and the Fort Mackinac Tea Room. For just a taste of the decadence, mini pecan balls are scooped at Sadie's Ice Cream Parlor, located at the east end of Grand Hotel.

286 Grand Ave., 906-847-3331
grandhotel.com

EAT LOCAL
WHITEFISH

The most conspicuous local flavors from Mackinac Island northward are fudge, pasties, and whitefish. Fudge needs no further introduction. Pasties (pronounced PASS-tees) are individual meat and root-vegetable pies wrapped in a flaky crust. They are filling, handheld meals that were convenient for miners to carry into Upper Peninsula copper mines, and they're still popular today. Because the UP is surrounded by three Great Lakes, fresh whitefish is plentiful. It's a popular menu item for its flaky texture and mild flavor, which lends itself to everything from dips and spreads to tacos and entrees.

A sampling of the variety of whitefish dishes on Mackinac Island:

Bistro on the Greens
Crisped whitefish sandwich with red cabbage slaw, lemon aioli

1 Lake Shore Rd., 906-847-3312
missionpoint.com

The Gate House
Whitefish bisque topped with garlic croutons and green onions

1547 Cadotte Ave., 906-847-3772
grandhotel.com

The Jockey Club
Parmesan-crusted whitefish with lobster ravioli

1874 Cadotte Ave., 906-847-9212
grandhotel.com

Millie's on Main
Salad of lemon-broiled whitefish with mixed greens and tomatoes

7294 Main St., 906-847-9901

milliesonmain.com

Pink Pony
Seared whitefish tacos with ginger dressing and avocado aioli

7221 Main St., 800-241-3341 or 906-847-3341

pinkponymackinac.com

Round Island Bar & Grill
Baked smoked whitefish dip with tomato jam and pita chips

1 Lake Shore Rd., 906-847-3000

missionpoint.com

Seabiscuit Café
Whitefish Reuben with coleslaw and Swiss cheese on marble rye

7337 Main St., 906-847-3611

seabiscuitcafe.com

TIP
Pasty shops and roadside pasty stands are plentiful across the Upper Peninsula. On Mackinac Island, head to Millie's on Main for this taste of the UP.

SUIT YOUR FOOD MOOD
AT MISSION POINT

There's a bounty of good eating at Mission Point Resort, from the rise-and-shine omelets expertly—and cheerily—made to order by longtime employee Sheldon to the truffle fries and grilled asparagus with aioli that will have you returning to Bistro on the Greens. At the family-friendly Round Island Bar & Grill, you can chow down indoors or out on elk chili, whitefish sandwiches, and Michigan cherry chicken salad with goat cheese. Piano music accompanies the fine dining at Chianti, where the menu features choice beef and select seafood, as well as Italian-influenced entrées and house-made pasta and marinara sauce (buy it by the jar from the resort's Boxwood Café). Retreat to the resort's Great Lawn level to Reserve, A Tasting Room for artisan cheese, charcuterie, and chocolate, along with the wines that complement them.

1 Lake Shore Rd., 906-847-3000
missionpoint.com

HANG
AT THE STANG

If the walls of the Mustang Lounge could talk, they'd be speaking French along with English, and not all stories from the hangout's colorful past would be appropriate in genteel company. Co-owners and buddies Tony Brodeur (the previous owner's grandson) and Jason Klonowski figure that the structure dates to the 1780s and likely belonged to a fur trader. They used two-hundred-year-old timbers in their remodel, and in addition to the Stang, they call it "Michigan's most historic tavern." The joint has been the go-to place for islanders, workers, and visitors since the 1940s and is one of only a few businesses open year-round. "Hang at the Stang" and have the Zing Zang Chili or grilled bacon mac 'n cheese sandwich, washed down with a Michigan beer or a Great Lakes lemonade.

1485 Astor St., 906-847-9916
mustang-lounge.com

SPEND AN ENCHANTING EVENING
IN THE WOODS

Tucked away in the forest like a storybook cottage, Woods Restaurant is a cozy spot for dinner in a setting that exudes Bavarian hunting lodge. Built as a children's playhouse by the owners of the adjacent Stonecliffe mansion (now an inn), the century-old chalet is decorated in warm red, yellow, and green, with antler chandeliers, taxidermy trophies, and crackling fireplaces. The red-gingham napkins and crayons for doodling on paper-topped tables lend a relaxed vibe, while white-jacketed waiters serving pork schnitzel, white onion soup, lamb shank, and raspberry crème brûlée leave no doubt this is a Grand Hotel dining experience. (Woods Restaurant welcomes hotel guests and non-guests. When making dinner reservations, be sure to discuss round-trip carriage transportation and allow time for a twenty-minute ride from Grand Hotel, more from elsewhere.)

8655 Cudahy Cir., 906-847-3699
grandhotel.com

TIP
Stop in at Woods for refreshments at Bobby's Bar, and roll a game on the oldest duckpin bowling alley in the country.

MAKE TIME FOR TEA TIME
AT GRAND HOTEL

Lovely harp music drifts through the parlor as hot tea is poured and champagne glasses clink. Tuxedoed servers deliver plates of open-faced cucumber sandwiches and precisely shaped, layered finger sandwiches. An assortment of Instagram-worthy sweets appears: scones, pastel macarons, pastries, chocolate-dipped strawberries, and petite, mousse-filled chocolate cups. More champagne, or a sherry, perhaps? Parents with young children, couples, groups of girlfriends, a mother and adult daughter, and Red Hat Ladies sip while savoring the array of treats. Conversations are low, the better to appreciate the sweet musical accompaniment to the relaxed and surprisingly unstuffy custom of afternoon tea at Grand Hotel.

286 Grand Ave., 906-847-3331
grandhotel.com

PACK A
PICNIC

Toting a picnic to someplace scenic is a tradition as old as fudge on Mackinac Island. You may opt to carry your feast to the island, or check with your hotel about ordering a box lunch, or swing by a convenient grab-and-go spot for ready-made eats. Picnic tables dot the island and are marked on the tourism bureau's free map. Bring a blanket to enjoy your spread on the lawn at Marquette Park or in a remote spot in the state park. Don't forget to rent a bicycle that has a basket to carry everything!

Bobby's Bar at Woods Restaurant
Boxed lunches and hot dogs

8655 Cudahy Cir., 906-847-3699
grandhotel.com

Boxwood Coffeeshop & Café
Freshly baked goods, sandwiches, charcuterie, beer, wine

1 Lake Shore Rd., 906-847-3000
missionpoint.com

Doud's Market and Doud's Market and Deli
To-go sandwiches, salads, snacks, and beverages at the full-service grocery store on Main and Fort Streets and the Main Street deli at the ferry docks.

7200 Main St. and 7395 Main St.
906-847-3444
doudsmarket.com

TIP

Pick up the suitable-for-framing map of "Favorite Picnic Spots of Mackinac Island," illustrated by local artist Kate Dupre, at Little Luxuries of Mackinac Island on Main Street.

7372-107 Main St., 906-847-9980
littleluxuriesofmackinac.com

UNWIND AND DINE WATERSIDE
AT CARRIAGE HOUSE

Follow the lush, garden-lined path to the waterfront dining room and outdoor veranda at the Hotel Iroquois, where the Carriage House serves views of Round Island Lighthouse and nightly piano entertainment with its classic American fare. The dinner menu of about ten entrées features seafood and steaks, and the Lake Superior whitefish is simply prepared with a special ingredient: the broiler pans that have been in use at the third-generation, family-owned Iroquois for six decades. Lunch offers a choice of soups, salads, and sandwiches, such as the Italian chopped salad and The Best BLT. Both of those appear on the condensed Verandah menu that's served at harbor-side umbrella tables between lunch and dinner. Save room for dessert with house-made hot fudge or an ice cream drink for adults.

7485 Main St., 906-847-3321
iroquoishotel.com

MIX IT UP
AT MISSION POINT

In a courtyard garden at Mission Point Resort, colorful perennials bloom alongside herbs and edible flowers. Pretty and practical, the mint, rosemary, sage, nasturtium, and other plants from the Cocktail Garden are destined to enhance libations as garnishes and house-made infusions, syrups, and bitters. Mission Point's mixologists not only concoct the cocktails but also share their expertise with guests in fun and educational "Garden to Glass" classes. The mixology sessions include a tour of the garden and tips on incorporating fresh herbs into cocktails and mocktails, such as the basil that is key to the house's Cocktail Garden Gimlet, made with Michigan's New Holland Knickerbocker Gin. Fresh mint leaves are muddled in a mojito, and lavender, hibiscus, and lemons combine for a refreshing take on lemonade, with or without the vodka.

1 Lake Shore Rd., 906-847-3000
missionpoint.com

FOLLOW YOUR NOSE
TO ICE HOUSE BBQ

It's a best-kept secret that can't last for long. Ice House BBQ is the only restaurant on the island that specializes in barbecue, and although it's hidden behind the Island House Hotel, there's no hiding the aroma of meat, smoked onsite daily, that drifts to Main Street and the marina across the way. Chickens are smoked whole, and baby back-ribs are dry rubbed and smoked for twelve hours, then finished on the grill. Pulled pork and brisket are served with a choice of traditional sides and appear in sandwiches, tacos, and chili. It's a new concept for the historic Island House, which opened in 1852 as one of the first summer resort hotels on Mackinac. Look for the Ice House BBQ sign at the walkway that leads to the rear of the property. Or just follow your nose.

TIP
The restaurant name pays homage to the ice harvesting industry of the 1800s, when the thick ice surrounding the island was cut into blocks of up to three hundred pounds, packed in sawdust, and stored in the ice house until it was needed in the summer months.

PUT ELEVEN PIECES OF SILVER TO USE
AT GRAND HOTEL

Gold letters spell *Salle à Manger* at the entrance to the main dining room, the gathering spot for Grand Hotel guests since 1887. Overlooking the Straits of Mackinac, it's an enormous space decorated in a garden of bright colors and bold green and white stripes, a beehive of activity where an impeccably dressed staff serves up to four thousand meals a day. Most guests are on the Modified American Plan and sit down for breakfast and dinner daily. The Grand Luncheon Buffet is popular with visitors who want to sample the resort experience without staying overnight. After 6:30 p.m., the Grand Hotel Orchestra provides accompaniment as guests arrive, dressed in finery befitting a meal that requires an eleven-piece silver setting. The leisurely dinner might include smoked duck breast, lobster bisque, rack of lamb, flourless bourbon chocolate cake, and, certainly, memories to savor.

286 Grand Ave., 906-847-3331
grandhotel.com

MUSIC AND ENTERTAINMENT

ROCK ON
AT THE WATER'S EDGE

Along the island's stony shoreline you'll see rocks carefully arranged in stacks small and tall, some more artfully than others. For centuries, cairns like these have served as shrines and landmarks, as trail markers, and to identify graves. The stacking of stones along Mackinac Island's Lake Shore Road seems mainly to be a diversion from bicycling—a chance to spend a little time at the water's edge, having fun with the challenge of building pillars that don't topple. It can be a solitary pursuit, a couple's or family activity, a meditative exercise, practice in mindfulness, a means of connecting with the environment, or just a way to leave a temporary mark on the world.

WALK
ON THE WILDFLOWER SIDE

Springtime, especially, is the season for wildflowers on the island, where botanists have identified about six hundred species of uncultivated, freely growing plants. Of those, 270 qualify as wildflowers, including trillium, dwarf lake iris, lady slipper, wild columbine, goldenrod, and Dutchman's breeches. Pick up a copy of the pamphlet "Checklist of Wildflowers of Mackinac Island" to record the variety you encounter on a walk in the woods, and imagine that you're following in the footsteps of Henry David Thoreau. The writer spent several days on the island in the summer of 1861, seeking relief and a restorative environment as he suffered from consumption (tuberculosis). Notes that he made while on Mackinac include a four-page list of plants and flowers he observed.

906-847-3328
mackinacparks.com

TIP
Take photos, not plant cuttings. Wildflowers on Michigan public lands are protected.

KICK BACK
IN MARQUETTE PARK

On the expansive green lawn below Fort Mackinac, where nineteenth-century soldiers dug potatoes and tended their vegetable garden, families now spread blankets for picnics, teens play Frisbee, photographers snap lilac blooms, couples marry, and kids scramble over the playscape. Bordering Main Street, across from the marina and Haldimand Bay, Marquette Park is a prime spot for observing the hustle and bustle while soaking up the sun under the gaze of the statue of its namesake, French explorer and Jesuit missionary Père Jacques Marquette. At the east end of the park, a bronze sculpture by Gareth Curtiss depicts a Native American figure rising from a turtle representing Mackinac Island. *Be Still* is the centerpiece of the Peace Garden that recognizes the friendly relationship between the United States and Canada following the War of 1812.

Main St., 906-847-3328
mackinacparks.com

TIP
Bring a blanket and relax on the lawn for the free Music in the Park concerts at 7 p.m. on summertime Thursdays.
906-984-4124, mackinacartscouncil.org

HEAR THE REST OF THE STORY
FROM MACKINAC REVEALED

Interested in the Victorian architecture of the bluff cottages and what's beyond the picket fences and porches? Curious about the flora and fauna of the woods that make up most of Mackinac? Looking for the lowdown on the lifestyles of year-round islanders? Join Moira Croghan on her Mackinac Revealed tour for insider knowledge of the place her family has called home since the 1800s. Learn about early island history, the geology and natural environment, and what it's really like to live motor vehicle-free. Small-group walking tours are regularly scheduled, and private tours are available. Moira especially enjoys leading bicycle safaris so she can share favorite trails, secret caves, and hidden vistas that aren't on the maps, but that she knows inside and out.

231-622-4867
mackinacrevealed.com

TIP
Arrange a drive-it-yourself carriage from Jack's Livery and turn the reins over to Moira for a special, private tour guided by an experienced horsewoman.

SEE THE SIGHTS
WITH MACKINAC ISLAND CARRIAGE TOURS

It was the nineteenth-century carriagemen—those who built carriages and operated horse-drawn transport services—who were behind the ban on the "dangerous horseless carriages" that sputtered onto the island, frightening the four-legged horsepower. Since 1898 their livelihoods have been safe, and the absence of motor vehicles is a big part of what makes Mackinac so special. In a bit less than two hours aboard a narrated Mackinac Island Carriage Tour, you'll get oriented to the lay of the land and its history and see some of the sights that contribute to the island's designation as a National Historic Landmark. The first tour of the day starts at 9 a.m., with the cheery red and yellow carriages departing the Main Street ticket office as they fill. Private carriage tours may be arranged by calling 906-847-3325.

7278 Main St., 906-847-3307
mict.com

TIP
Wheelchair or scooter users are asked to call at least forty-eight hours in advance to check on availability of a handicapped-accessible carriage.

CHECK OUT
THE PUBLIC LIBRARY

Spending precious vacation time in a public library isn't such a curious idea when the setting is as lovely as that of Mackinac Island's, set on the waterfront at Biddle Point. The soft mint-green exterior is the first clue that there's something special behind its classically pillared façade. Carleton Varney's interior design doesn't disappoint, with brilliant colors, a chandelier, art tiles on the wood-burning fireplace, and windows framing views of Round Island Lighthouse. Book loans are reserved for residents, but you can select something from the ongoing used book sale and settle into one of the Adirondack chairs on the deck for a relaxing read just steps from the lake. Each summer you're invited to enjoy the free author series, art exhibits, and special programs—no library card required.

7549 Main St., 906-847-3421
uproc.lib.mi.us/mackisle

FLUTTER BY
TO SEE BUTTERFLIES

Mackinac Island is home to not one but two butterfly attractions, where you can stroll among fascinating flying insects from North America and around the world. The Original Butterfly House and Insect World opened in 1991, just behind Ste. Anne Catholic Church at the east end of Main Street. Wings of Mackinac Butterfly Conservatory is located up the hill near the Grand Hotel Stables. At both indoor gardens, keep the camera ready for photo ops as the colorful creatures flutter freely, alighting on multiple feeding stations, flowering plants, and visitors. You may even see butterflies emerge from their chrysalides. Each spot has a gift shop and special displays: Butterfly House dedicates a gallery to a variety of insects, and kids love the fairy garden at Wings of Mackinac.

The Original Butterfly House and Insect World
6750 McGulpin St., 906-847-3972
originalbutterflyhouse.com

Wings of Mackinac Butterfly Conservatory
7528 Carriage Rd., 906-847-9464
wingsofmackinac.com

TIP

Visitors may witness the arrival in early
summer of monarch butterflies that migrate
to Mackinac from Mexico to reproduce.
In late summer their offspring then wing
it two thousand miles south for the winter,
and the cycle is repeated the following year.

SLIP AWAY
ON A SLEEK YACHT

Feel the fresh, clean air that fills the billowing sails, and let the rhythm of the sweetwater sea lull you into a state of pure relaxation on a laidback sail in the Straits of Mackinac. If you prefer, Captain Dave Berger welcomes you to take the wheel of his fifty-foot sailboat, 50 Free, on a two-hour scheduled daytime or sunset sailing adventure with SailMackinac. Or book a custom two- to four-hour outing with Captain David Rowe aboard his Wild Honey Sailing Charters' Cal 39 sloop. Both boats can accommodate up to six passengers for a memorable Mackinac sailing experience.

SailMackinac
517-712-6918
sailmackinac.com

Wild Honey Sailing Charters
810-516-5052
sailwildhoney.com

HAVE AN ARTFUL TIME
WITH THE MACKINAC ARTS COUNCIL

An engraved plate marks the red velvet chair in the Mission Point Theater where actor Christopher Reeve sat, mesmerized by Jane Seymour's character in the 1980 film *Somewhere in Time*. You could settle into that seat for a movie screening or concert sponsored by the Mackinac Arts Council, which supports arts programming and events for the enjoyment of residents and visitors, including changing exhibits at the Center for the Arts gallery. The nonprofit organization brings live performances to several venues on the island and hosts the free Music in the Park series on Thursday evenings at Marquette Park. If you're inspired by Mackinac's beauty, you can express yourself at an art workshop at the Mackinac Art Museum, where local artists share their talents in drawing, plein air painting, bead weaving, calligraphy, and photography.

Center for the Arts
6633 Main St., 906-984-4124
mackinacartscouncil.org

DRINK IN THE SCENERY
ABOARD SIP N' SAIL CRUISES

Soak up the Straits of Mackinac views while enjoying refreshments, music, and memory making on a scheduled themed or chartered excursion aboard the classic *Isle Royale Queen III*. The eighty-one-foot vessel has a long history of service on the Great Lakes, originally ferrying passengers across Lake Superior between Copper Harbor and Isle Royale National Park. The *Queen III* is comfortably outfitted with indoor seating, a lounge on the outdoor deck, and a full-service bar. Salute the day with a Bloody Mary, or sip a Michigan microbrew on a craft beer cruise. Take in the sights on the Great Turtle Voyage, or catch the ooh-and-aah-some Fourth of July fireworks cruise.

Arnold Freight/Coal Dock, 844-906-9006
puremichiganboatcruises.com

TIP
Tickets must be purchased in advance, online only.

GARDEN GAWK
ON A BIKE RIDE OR WALK

The naturally slower pace of a place where getting around is by foot, bicycle, or carriage makes it easy to absorb the beauty of the island's bountiful garden beds and borders, hanging baskets, and window boxes. Throughout its short season, Mackinac is a riot of color and variety of blooms, bulbs, herbs, ornamental grasses, ground covers, shrubs, hedges, and topiary. Landscapes integrate existing rocks and boulders and incorporate arbors, dry-stacked rock walls, and decorative gates for interest. It's called "the Mackinac Island look" by Jack Barnwell, whose landscape company creates and maintains hundreds of projects each year. The results are even more impressive when you remember that all that bloomin' material is moved, and the work is done, without the aid of motorized transport or maintenance equipment.

TIP
Guided walking tours of private cottage gardens are a highlight of the annual Grand Garden Show. The August event is hosted at Grand Hotel by Proven Winners, noted supplier of annuals, perennials, and shrubs, with gardening guru Jack Barnwell. Overnight packages and day-attendance tickets are available.
815-899-1973, grandgardenshow.com

TWIRL AROUND
THE TERRACE ROOM FLOOR

Since Grand Hotel's early years, live music has been an important part of entertaining and amusing guests, from orchestras performing on the porch and lawn to formal dances. That custom continues, and each day from noon until nearly midnight, guests may enjoy the talents of professional musicians in at least one area of the resort. Almost every evening at 9:30, the doors of the Terrace Room swing open and the Grand Hotel Orchestra takes the stage, enticing gentlemen in suits and ties and ladies in their dressy attire to step out onto the parquet floor to experience dancing in the grand tradition.

286 Grand Ave., 906-847-3331
grandhotel.com

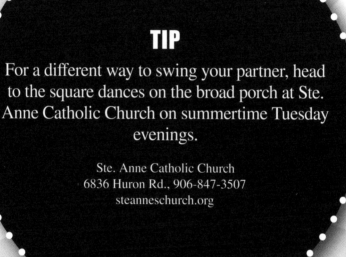

TIP

For a different way to swing your partner, head to the square dances on the broad porch at Ste. Anne Catholic Church on summertime Tuesday evenings.

Ste. Anne Catholic Church
6836 Huron Rd., 906-847-3507
steanneschurch.org

GET INTO THE SPIRIT
ON THE HAUNTS OF MACKINAC TOUR

An Army private hanged for murdering a superior at Fort Mackinac, a snubbed suitor, lost children, and suicide. This is the stuff of the ninety-minute Haunts of Mackinac guided walking tour that winds through downtown, with stops for stories about historical figures and events that are connected to strange sightings and unexplained happenings. The evening tours grew out of Todd Clements's book about the legends, tragic tales, and ghost stories of Mackinac Island. With its history as a Native American spiritual place and burial ground, military fort, and battlefield, there's enough material for a tour that's more informative than scary. Except for the creepy phantom bicyclist with empty eye sockets. On a dark and drizzly Mackinac night, it's easy to imagine that any one of the passing bicyclists could be that guy.

7416 Main St., 906-847-8018
hauntsofmackinac.com

HAVE A GOOD OLDE TYME
AT HORN'S GASLIGHT

To experience Mackinac Island's pub culture, head to Horn's. When Prohibition ended in 1933, Edward and Violet Horn landed one of the first liquor licenses in Michigan and transformed their pool hall and snack shop into Horn's Gaslight Bar. Still in the family, Horn's Gaslight Bar & Restaurant retains an old-timey saloon feel, with its pressed-tin ceiling and gorgeous back bar. The lunchtime menu of burgers and sandwiches shifts into Southwestern/Mexican mode in the evening, with a half-dozen margaritas to complement the Tex-Mex flavors. After the last ferry of the day has left the island and the band takes the stage, the dance floor is packed until closing time.

7300 Main St., 906-847-6154
hornsbar.com

TIP
Live music is an important part of the social scene on the island, and you'll find entertainment at multiple bars and restaurants just about every night of the week.

GAZE UPON THE BEAUTIFUL PANORAMA
AT THE CUPOLA BAR

The prominent cupola that crowns Grand Hotel was an open-air pavilion when the resort first welcomed guests in 1887. A newspaper reporter described it as "capable of holding a large number of persons . . . from which can be seen one of the most beautiful panoramas nature has ever spread out for man to gaze upon." The landmark architectural feature was renovated for the Grand Hotel centennial and opened in 1987 as the Cupola Bar. Salute the sun as it sinks beyond the Mackinac Bridge, or sip a nightcap to soft piano music as the stars come out, all while gazing through the banks of windows that wrap around the room. Carleton Varney chose an elaborate Venetian glass chandelier as the centerpiece of the two-story space, but even it can't compete with the panoramic view of the Straits of Mackinac.

286 Grand Ave., 906-847-3331
grandhotel.com

FIND SCENTSATIONAL FUN
AT THE LILAC FESTIVAL

Since before the Civil War, the fragrance of lilacs has filled the summertime air on Mackinac Island, where growing conditions suit the flowering shrubs that blossom in shades of purple, pink, white, and even yellow. Henry David Thoreau, on a visit in 1861, made the first known written acknowledgment of lilacs on the island. Each June since 1949, the Mackinac Island Lilac Festival has celebrated the thousands of blooms that are as much a part of the landscape as the Victorian cottages and horse-drawn carriages. The ten-day event appeals to all senses, with concerts, food and beverage tastings, a 10K run, and walking tours with a lilac expert. Representatives of local Native American tribes lead the Lilac Festival Grand Parade, in which the Lilac Queen—and purple—reign.

906-847-3783
mackinacisland.org

TRAVEL
SOMEWHERE IN TIME

The 1980 film *Somewhere in Time* starring Jane Seymour as actress Elise McKenna and Christopher Reeve as Richard Collier, the playwright who loves her, was set in and around Grand Hotel and filmed largely on Mackinac Island. The time-travel tearjerker inspires fans of the romantic tale, based on the book *Bid Time Return* by Richard Matheson, to attend the Grand Hotel Somewhere in Time Weekend each October. Guests engage in discussions about the production, view a special screening of the film, and dress in elaborate, 1912-appropriate clothing for a luncheon buffet, cocktail receptions, and the Costume Promenade. Grand Hotel makes the movie available for guest viewing throughout the season, and one of its suites is dedicated to *Somewhere in Time*.

286 Grand Ave., 906-847-3331
grandhotel.com

TIP
Favorite film locations always accessible to fans include the *Somewhere in Time* gazebo, located behind and east of Fort Mackinac, and the lakeside "Is it you?" spot where the couple met; look for the plaque along M-185 near mile marker seven.

CATCH THE SUNRISE,
WATCH THE SUNSET

Stay at least one night on Mackinac Island and you'll discover there's something magical about its mornings—early mornings, as the sun is just beginning to light the sky, well before the first ferry arrives at the dock, as the nearly empty Main Street is hosed down before the crowds arrive. When it's so quiet you can hear the clip-clop of a dray team mixing with the whirring sound of bicycles as workers head to their posts. Late in the day is special, too, when crowds thin with each ferry departure, shopkeepers flip "open" signs to "closed," street lights flicker on, and music wafts from bars and restaurants. Plan to catch sunrise from Mission Point's Great Lawn or Robinson's Folly, and watch the setting sun at British Landing or Sunset (a.k.a. Chimney) Rock.

TIP
Great Turtle Kayak offers kayak and paddleboard tours to Arch Rock at sunrise and Devil's Kitchen at sunset.
7395 Main St., 231-715-2925, mackinackayak.com

JUST SAY SPAAAAHHHH
AT MISSION POINT RESORT

As if the slow pace of Mackinac Island isn't enough to calm the frazzled visitor, Mission Point Resort offers Lakeside Spa and Salon, a full-service sanctuary in a soothing palette of neutral colors and with a mix of natural materials, contemporary furnishings, antiques, and local art. There are treatment rooms for singles and couples, saunas and steam rooms, spacious locker and dressing areas, and a salon space outfitted with multiple pampering stations popular with bridal parties. The spa's signature Lilac Facial and Body Treatment uses lilac essential oil, and the Freshwater Lake Huron Spa Package includes a stone massage. Spa guests also have access to the adjacent fitness center.

1 Lake Shore Rd., 800-833-5583
missionpoint.com

TIP

There are two additional spas on
Mackinac Island:

Astor's Salon and Spa
286 Grand Ave., 906-847-3331
grandhotel.com

Lilac Tree Spa
7372 Main St., 906-847-9171
lilactree.com

PORCH SIT
AT GRAND HOTEL

You may have seen or heard about the world's longest porch, the 660-foot, columned veranda that fronts Grand Hotel. From the resort's opening in 1887, the porch has been a gathering place for socializing, "flirtation walks," and admiring the view of the Straits of Mackinac. The first public demonstration of Thomas Edison's phonograph was held on the porch, and presidents and other dignitaries have walked its width. Rimmed with lattice flower boxes filled with Grand Hotel's signature red geraniums, it's lined with one hundred white wooden rocking chairs that invite sitting, reading, conversing, dozing, and sipping a beverage. If you're not a guest at Grand Hotel, you'll be charged a ten-dollar fee to visit the National Historic Landmark to enjoy some of its amenities, including a perch on the legendary porch.

286 Grand Ave., 906-847-3331
grandhotel.com

TIP

Visitors who pay the ten-dollar fee may apply that amount to the cost of the Grand Luncheon Buffet in the main dining room, shop at the variety of boutiques, admire the exhibit at the Grand Art Gallery, and stroll the gardens and grounds, including the hidden labyrinth.

SPORTS AND RECREATION

GO AROUND IN CIRCLES
ON THE CAR-FREE HIGHWAY

Here's your chance to travel the only state highway in the country that bans motor vehicles, the paved M-185 that follows the Lake Huron shoreline in a gentle, 8.2-mile loop around the island. A yellow dividing line mostly succeeds in keeping bicyclists, carriages, pedestrians, and runners in their own lanes, even as they're distracted by scenic views of passing boat traffic and the Mackinac Bridge. The highway is called Main Street through town and becomes Lake Shore Road for much of the circular route. Pack a snack and water, and plan to stop along the way at picnic tables and scenic and historic sites, including British Landing, the halfway (and restroom) spot.

TIP
Locals recommend traveling the path in both clockwise and counterclockwise directions, not because they like to see fudgies going around in circles, but because the views are different and spectacular each way.

PUT YOUR
METTLE TO THE PEDAL

Whether you're an avid cyclist or haven't straddled a saddle seat in oh, a few years, when on Mackinac, do as the islanders do and two-wheel it. Bicycling is the quickest way to get around and affords the freedom of exploring remote areas of the island that are detailed in the tourism bureau map and the Mackinac Historic State Parks' "Historic Mackinac Island Visitor's Guide." After a spin around the 8.2-mile paved perimeter road, head uphill (you won't be the only one walking your bike) to experience the island's interior beauty. Enjoy a quiet ride through the woods, stunning views of the Straits of Mackinac, historic sites, and natural wonders along seventy-plus miles of trails, including some that challenge mountain bikers.

PADDLE THE INLAND SEA
WITH GREAT TURTLE KAYAK

Lake Huron's crystal-clear waters lap the shore, inviting exploration of the Straits of Mackinac. Never mind that you've never kayaked or haven't paddled since that canoe trip with the scouts. Bring your waterproof camera and let Great Turtle Kayak Tours take you on a memorable sunrise, sunset, or midday outing to view the island's coastline, geological formations, and Victorian architecture from a new perspective. Expert guides lead small groups of single or tandem kayakers and stand-up paddleboarders on half- to two-hour excursions for adventurers of all skill levels. More experienced paddlers may circumnavigate the island or venture across the Straits of Mackinac to explore Bois Blanc Island and uninhabited Round Island, famous for its red and white lighthouse.

7395 Main St., 231-715-2925
mackinackayak.com

TIP
Make it a camping trip. Pack your sleeping bag and Great Turtle will provide the rest of the gear for an overnight stay on Round Island or Bois Blanc Island.

GIVE STONE SKIPPING
A SPIN

Gather your six best flat-bottomed, nicely weighted stones and head to Windermere Point for the Mackinac Island International Stone Skipping and Gerplunking Competition, held on July 4 of each year since 1969. Little kids get started by lobbing rocks into the water for the best "gerplunk" sound, and stone-skipping youth twelve and under compete in the Pebbles Division. Amateurs (age thirteen and up) may qualify to compete against world record holders in the main event, the Wilmer T. Rabe Pro-Invitational International Stone Skipping Tournament. Hundreds of spectators line the rocky shore to watch as each entrant makes a half-dozen attempts to achieve the highest number of skips (usually in the range of twenty-six to thirty-one skips). Winners receive trophies and a year's supply of Ryba's Fudge.

stoneskipping.com

TIP
If you don't know your pitty-pats from your plinks and plonks, show up at 10 a.m.-ish for the pre-competition Stone Skipping Clinic, where you can get pointers from the pros.

GET THE WHEEL DEAL
ON GETTING AROUND

Bicycle rental outfits lining Main Street will match you with the right wheels for your excursion, whether you plan to cruise the paved perimeter road or hit the rougher inland trails. You'll find single- and multi-speed, tandem, mountain and fat tire bikes, adult tricycles, and tow-alongs for kids, plus strollers, wheelchairs, and mobility carts. (Golf carts are restricted to golf courses; ATV/ORVs are prohibited on the island.) Bring your own bike for a ferry fee of about ten dollars, or roll like a local and get a $3.50 bicycle license for free transport. You'll have to plan ahead so the license can be mailed to you before your trip; phone 906-847-3345 for more info. Need service? Mackinac Wheels offers bike repairs and supplies.

TIP
Make sure your bike is equipped with fenders—you'll be sharing the roads with horses (use your imagination).

RENTAL COMPANIES

Island House Bike Shop
6966 Main St., 906-847-3347
theislandhouse.com

Mackinac Bike Barn
7411 Main St., 906-847-8026
mackinacbikes.com

Mackinac Cycle
7271 Main St., 906-847-0047
mackinaccycle.com

Mackinac Island Bike Shop
7421 Main St., 906-847-6337
bikemackinac.com

Mackinac Island Mobility Center
7439 Main St., 906-847-6337
bikemackinac.com

Mackinac Wheels
6929 Main St., 906-847-8022
mackinacbikes.com

Ryba's Bicycle Rentals
7245 Main St. and 7463 Main St., 906-847-3208
rybabikes.com

MAKE A SPLASH
AT GRAND HOTEL

You don't have to be a Grand Hotel guest to enjoy the resort's beautiful, serpentine outdoor swimming pool and its amenities. While free to those staying at the resort, the Esther Williams Swimming Pool is open to other visitors for a daily fee (except on the Fourth of July and Labor Day weekend). The pool is named for the competitive swimmer and actress who starred in *This Time for Keeps*, a 1947 movie filmed at Grand Hotel. Lounge chairs line the deck of the 220-foot, 500,000-gallon pool, and the facility includes two whirlpools and a sauna. Kids love the pool toys and free snow cones, and the convenient Pool Grill serves food and beverages.

286 Grand Ave., 906-847-3331
grandhotel.com

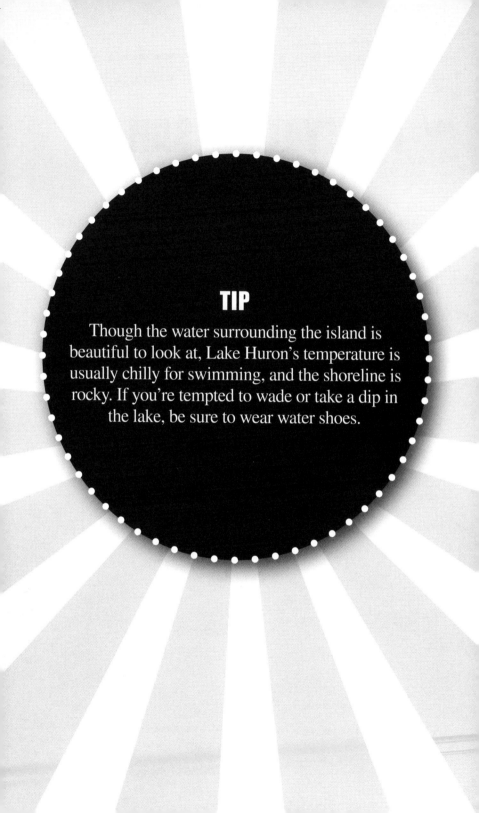

TIP

Though the water surrounding the island is beautiful to look at, Lake Huron's temperature is usually chilly for swimming, and the shoreline is rocky. If you're tempted to wade or take a dip in the lake, be sure to wear water shoes.

PARTY LIKE A SAILOR
AFTER A LEGENDARY RACE

You don't need sea legs to appreciate the skill and spectacle of the freshwater sailboat competitions that bookend one summer week each July, when the Chicago Yacht Club Race to Mackinac crosses Lake Michigan and the Bayview to Mackinac Race sails from Port Huron to the finish line at Round Island Lighthouse. From five entries in its inaugural 1898 race, Chicago's by-invitation competition now draws about 320 boats and 3,200 crew members. The Port Huron event, held annually since 1925, attracts two hundred boats crewed by two thousand. Friends, family, and spectators cheer arriving boats and toast their marathon efforts at post-race celebrations. The excitement of the competition, the sight of hundreds of boats filling the harbor, and swarms of sailing buffs make the Mackinac races festive traditions that even landlubbers love.

Bayview Yacht Club Mackinac Race
bycmack.com

Chicago Yacht Club Race to Mackinac
cycracetomackinac.com

STRAITS RACES

All sailboats and skill levels are welcome to participate in four annual races in the Straits of Mackinac. Each event is followed by an awards party at the Mackinac Island Yacht Club.

July: Pink Pony Fourth of July Sailboat Race
July: Round the Island Race
August: Mission Point Mac to Mac Regatta
September: Horn's Bar Labor Day Regatta

Mackinac Island Yacht Club
7006 Main St., 906-847-3363
miyachtclub.com

• •

TIP

No sailboat? No problem. You and your crew of five friends can compete aboard a chartered fifty-foot custom offshore racing yacht with SailMackinac.

517-712-6918
sailmackinac.com

BYO HORSE
TO THE EQUINE B&B

Sure, there are saddle horses and self-drive carriages for rent, but imagine the joy of riding your own horse on car-free Mackinac Island, exploring the forty miles of bridle paths and trails, following the shoreline roadway, and splashing in Lake Huron's waters. Bring and board your horse at the Mackinac Community Equestrian Center's handsome thirteen-stall stable, situated on more than three acres of former farmland. Guests get fresh hay and daily stall cleaning, tack storage, and use of the one-hundred-by-two-hundred-foot outdoor arena. Best availability for horse boarding is in June, September, and October; ferry transport for horses is from St. Ignace, in the Upper Peninsula. See the website for guidelines, requirements, tips, and suggestions for spending time with your steed on Mackinac Island, where "horse is king."

3800 British Landing Rd., 906-847-8034
mackinachorses.org

TIP
The Mackinac Horsemen's Association advises that you first visit the island without your horse, so that you're comfortable with the unique challenges inherent to the island's many bicycles, carriages, wagons, and crowds of pedestrians.

CRUISE INTO
HALDIMAND BAY

Standing at the water's edge, an eight-foot-tall replica of the Statue of Liberty, one of two hundred presented across the United States by the Boy Scouts of America in 1950, welcomes boaters to the Mackinac Island State Harbor at Haldimand Bay. The Michigan Department of Natural Resources manages the busy Lake Huron harbor and handles reservations for the eighty-slip marina, which accommodates boats of up to seventy feet. Amenities include restrooms, showers, water, electricity (30 and 50 amp), and Wi-Fi; grills and picnic tables; a dog run; pumpout, refuse, and recycle receptacles; nearby fuel; and US Customs check-in. Conveniently located to downtown's restaurants, shops, and attractions, it's directly across from the greenspace at Marquette Park and the whitewashed Fort Mackinac on the bluff above.

906-847-3561
midnrreservations.com

TIP
Request a well on the outer side of the T-shaped dock; with bow pointed toward land you'll enjoy views of Fort Mackinac and a bit of distance and privacy from the passing Main Street traffic.

DIVE WRECKS AND ROCKS
IN THE STRAITS OF MACKINAC

The waters of lakes Huron and Michigan challenged nineteenth-century captains navigating channels and islands while dealing with storms, fog, and ice. The 148-square-mile area that stretches from the north side of Mackinac Island and around the Lower Peninsula coastline is strewn with a dozen lost vessels resting in depths of 40 to 150 feet. All are wooden boats from the 1800s, except the 604-foot steel freighter *Cedarville*, which went down in 1965. Remains of all shipwrecks are protected by the Straits of Mackinac Shipwreck Preserve, one of fourteen Michigan Underwater Preserves that promote maritime history and diver access to the sites and provide underwater resources, information, and links to area dive shops and charter boat operators.

Straits of Mackinac Shipwreck Preserve
straitspreserve.com

Michigan Underwater Preserves
800-970-8717
michiganpreserves.org

TIP

Scuba divers also like to explore ancient breccia formations off the Mackinac Island shore, including the Rock Maze (good to snorkel) and Mackinac Falls, a one-hundred-foot waterfall that was discovered in 2007.

SADDLE UP
FOR A RIDE TO REMEMBER

Horsepower of the four-legged kind is an unforgettable way to experience the wooded trails of Mackinac Island State Park. Cindy's Riding Stable and Jack's Livery Stable, each fourth-generation family businesses, match your riding ability with one of their saddle horses and provide basic instructions so that even newbies can join one of the leisurely guided trail rides. More skilled riders may opt for independent exploration of the park's forty miles of bridle trails and paths that take you far from the bustle of Main Street and the downtown area. (Saddle horses are for ages ten and up; some other restrictions apply.)

Cindy's Riding Stable
7447 Market St., 906-847-3572
cindysridingstable.com

Jack's Livery Stable
7754 Mahoney Ave., 906-847-3391
jacksliverystable.com

DRIVE YOUR OWN
HORSE AND BUGGY

Take the reins of a horse-drawn buggy from Jack's Livery Stable and enjoy the freedom and charm of a self-guided carriage tour of Mackinac Island—no experience required! Clip-clop along the perimeter Lake Shore Road or follow park roads through the woods on a romantic ride for two or a family outing for up to six passengers. Jack's is a fourth-generation business with a stable of horses that the knowledgeable staff matches to your level of expertise. You'll receive brief driving instructions, horse-handling tips, a map, and suggested routes based on your interests and length of outing.

7754 Mahoney Ave., 906-847-3391
jacksliverystable.com

HAVE A REEL GOOD TIME
ON A FISHING CHARTER

Experience the thrill of landing your dinner straight from the Great Lakes on a charter fishing excursion. Captain Dennis Gorsuch of E.U.P. Fishing Charters and Captain Chris Becker of North Shore Sport Fishing Charters know where to find lake trout, steelhead trout, king salmon, and Atlantic salmon on half- or full-day outings for up to six anglers, including kids. They'll pick you up at Mackinac Island in their comfortable sport fishing boats and supply all the necessary gear; you can even purchase your fishing license on board. Ask the captain to clean and fillet your catch and to share the names of local chefs who'll cook it for you.

E.U.P. Fishing Charters
251-504-1046
eupfishingcharters.net

North Shore Sport Fishing Charters
906-430-2839
northshoresportfishingcharter.com

GO FLY
A KITE

Every day (weather permitting), colorful kites fill the sky at Windermere Point, welcoming arriving ferries and, hopes Great Turtle Toys store owner Ben Nye, enticing visitors of all ages to try their hand at kite flying. He's on a mission to spread the high-flying fun, and his staff welcomes you to try the demonstration kites, which range from the easy-to-fly, triangular delta to box kites and dragon kites that unfurl to 150 feet long. Great Turtle Toys carries kites suitable for beginner and intermediate flyers, as well as some advanced, high-tech models. You can also bring your own kites to test the island's shifting winds, which can be unpredictable and make for a fun challenge.

Great Turtle Toys
7372 Main St., 906-847-6118
greatturtletoys.com

TIP
In addition to Windermere Point, the island's safest spots for flying kites are Great Turtle Park, the Mackinac Island Public School grounds, and the Great Lawn at Mission Point Resort.

TAKE A SWING
AT MACKINAC GOLF

Golfers have a choice of distinctively different experiences within Mackinac Island's 3.8 square miles, including a rare example of a nineteenth-century course at Wawashkamo Golf Club. The nine-hole links course has changed little since it was laid out in 1898 by Scotsman Alex Smith on what was a War of 1812 battlefield. Wawashkamo, which means "walk a crooked trail," hosts the National Hickory Stick Classic each August and has hickories for rent. Grand Hotel's eighteen-hole Jewel requires a carriage ride between its Grand nine holes, with Straits of Mackinac views, and the Woods nine, a mile and a half away. At Mission Point Resort, the Greens of Mackinac is an eighteen-hole executive putting course with bent grass greens along the Lake Huron shore. It's open for daytime and evening glow golf fun.

The Jewel
1 Grand Ave., 906-847-9218
grandhotel.com

The Greens of Mackinac
1 Lake Shore Rd., 906-847-3000
missionpoint.com

Wawashkamo Golf Club
1 British Landing Rd., 906-847-3871
wawashkamo.com

TIP

Check the websites for packages that include golf, lodging, meals, and more.

SEE THE SIGHTS
OF THE COUNTRY'S
SECOND NATIONAL PARK

In a span of twenty years, Mackinac morphed from military outpost to being named, in 1875, the second US national park (after Yellowstone); in 1895, control was transferred from the federal government to the state, and it became Michigan's first state park. There is no fee to access Mackinac Island State Park, which covers more than eighty percent of the island. Pets are welcome, but camping, hunting, and campfires are prohibited. The park's seventy-plus miles of trails connect historic sites, scenic views, and natural geological wonders formed over millions of years. Mostly limestone bedrock, the island is covered with a thin layer of soil that manages to support 270 varieties of wildflowers, a coniferous forest, and a mixed hardwood forest. Its wildlife population includes birds, squirrels, chipmunks, rabbits, bats, and turtles, with a smattering of foxes, white-tailed deer, coyotes, and bobcats that sometimes cross from the mainland via ice bridges.

Mackinac Island State Park Visitor's Center
7165 Main St., 906-847-3328
mackinacparks.com

TIP

Stop at the Visitor's Center for an overview and tips on exploring the park. Pop for the inexpensive but handy "Historic Mackinac Island Visitor's Guide," which describes seven themed touring routes with maps.

GET A BIRD'S-EYE VIEW
WITH MACKINAW PARASAILING

Soar six hundred feet above the Straits of Mackinac on a parasail flight that's suitable for all ages—no experience required (certain restrictions apply). Just pull on the life vest, buckle up, sit back, relax, and enjoy the liftoff right from the deck of the Mackinaw Parasailing boat. Take in the spectacular views of the island, Mackinac Bridge, and boat traffic below. Each flight lasts ten to twelve minutes and can accommodate one, two, or three riders. Let the captain know if you want to get your feet wet, and he'll dip you down to lake level for a splash before landing. Observers can take the boat ride for a small fee. Advance reservations are suggested.

7271 Main St., 866-436-7144
mackinawparasailing.com

TIP
Enjoy a discounted rate for two on the 9 a.m.
Morning Eye Opener flight.

MAKE STRIDES
FOR MACKINAC FOOT RACES

Each year Run Mackinac organizes what it calls "Three Great Races, One Beautiful Island" for runners and walkers of all abilities, in June, September, and October.

LILAC 10K RUN AND WALK—This annual early-June Lilac Festival event draws more than one thousand participants, who race from the busy downtown, through the center of the island, and along scenic Lake Shore Road.

MACKINAC ISLAND EIGHT MILE—Now approaching a half-century of road races, this fairly flat, paved route around the island is a family-friendly event that attracts about two thousand walkers and runners each September.

GREAT TURTLE TRAIL RUN—A maximum of three thousand runners and walkers follow scenic inner-island trails during this annual, end-of-season October event, which features a half marathon and 5.7-mile run/walk.

runmackinac.com

ESCAPE
TO A SNOW-COVERED OASIS

Mackinac Island takes on a quiet, otherworldly quality when it's covered in white. The streets are nearly deserted, and just a couple of lodging and dining spots and shops are open for the winter. The ban on motorized vehicles is lifted, and the hum of snowmobiles fills the air. People-powered transport is by cross-country skis, snowshoes, and fat bikes with wide tires made for traveling on top of the snow, so you can easily cruise to the craggy limestone formations of Arch Rock and Sugar Loaf. Skaters will enjoy the state park's free outdoor ice rink behind Fort Mackinac. You must bring your own sports equipment, although a limited number of fat tire bikes are available for rent from Mackinac Wheels; be sure to phone ahead to reserve yours.

Mackinac Wheels
6929 Main St., 906-847-8022
mackinacbikes.com

TIP

The Twilight Turtle Trek is a free,
two-mile, lantern-lit cross-country ski
and snowshoe outing with bonfire and hot
chocolate in January, February, and March.
Check the schedule at mackinacparks.com.

SUIT UP
AND SNOWMOBILE

When snow blankets Mackinac, snowmobiles roar to life. It's the only time of year that the public is allowed to operate a motor vehicle on the island, and sledders look forward to buzzing about on their machines through picturesque streets, exploring state park trails, and circling M-185, the 8.2-mile perimeter road. Star Line will ferry your snowmobile from St. Ignace for a fee, based on availability. Sleds must be registered and display a snowmobile trail permit from the Michigan Department of Natural Resources. On arrival at the island, visitors must purchase a five-dollar snowmobile day pass at the head of the ice bridge, state park office, or police department.

Mackinac Island State Park Field Office
1856 Fort Service Rd., 906-847-6607
mackinacparks.com

Michigan DNR
517-284-6057
michigan.gov/dnr

Star Line Mackinac Island Ferry
800-638-9892
mackinacferry.com

TIP

By February, if the weather cooperates, thick
ice halts ferry service and an ice bridge forms
between the island and the Upper Peninsula.
Residents use Christmas trees to mark the route
between British Landing and St. Ignace.
However, because of changing, unpredictable
conditions, the ice bridge can be extremely
dangerous. Lives and sleds have been
lost. The US Coast Guard does
not condone crossing it.

PACK FIDO'S BAG
FOR MACKINAC

Mackinac Island welcomes well-behaved dogs on leashes—and owners who clean up after them. With more than eighty percent of its area designated as state park land, the island offers plenty of room to roam with four-legged friends on the seventy-plus miles of inner-island trails and 8.2-mile perimeter road. Dogs are welcome to visit Fort Mackinac and board the Mackinac Island Carriage Tours, where lap dogs ride free; there is a fee for larger dogs. Mission Point Resort is one of three dog-friendly lodging options on the island. For meals, pack picnics or ask restaurants with outdoor dining whether they permit pets on the patios (the Tea Room at Fort Mackinac is one). Bonus: pets ride free on the ferries.

Fort Mackinac
7127 Huron Rd., 906-847-3328
mackinacparks.com

Mackinac Island Carriage Tours
7278 Main St., 906-847-3307
mict.com

Mission Point Resort
1 Lake Shore Rd., 906-847-3000
missionpoint.com

Park Place Suites of Mackinac Island
7323 Market St., 906-430-7400
miparkplacesuites.com

Sunset Condominiums
8704 Eckel Dr., 906-847-3407
sunsetcondos.com

Shepler's Ferry
800-828-6157
sheplersferry.com

Star Line Mackinac Island Ferry
800-638-9892
mackinacferry.com

CULTURE AND HISTORY

LEAVE YOUR CARES
(AND CAR) BEHIND

Some of the fun of Mackinac Island is getting there. Most visitors arrive by passenger ferries that depart Mackinaw City, at the top of the Lower Peninsula, and St. Ignace, the gateway to the Upper Peninsula. Shepler's Ferry and Star Line Mackinac Island Ferry service both cities, where vehicle parking is ample and secure. The ferry ride is about twenty minutes long, and you're free to choose a seat on the open-air top deck or indoor lower deck. Reservations are not required but may be made online; look for discounts on tickets. Departures vary according to season; ferries do not run through the night. Both companies transport pets, bicycles, and strollers, and Star Line, which operates until wintry conditions and ice prohibit crossing, will convey your snowmobile for a fee.

Shepler's Ferry
800-828-6157, sheplersferry.com

Star Line Mackinac Island Ferry
800-638-9892, mackinacferry.com

TIP
Try to catch the ferry that makes a quick detour for a close-up view of the Mackinac Bridge, the twin-towered, five-mile suspension bridge that connects the upper and lower peninsulas.

Boaters are welcome at the Mackinac Island State Harbor (See page 61.)

Private and charter planes may land at Mackinac Island Airport's lighted, 3,500-foot paved runway. Great Lakes Air provides charter service from St. Ignace; reservations are required for the four-minute flight aboard the single engine Cherokee 6.

Great Lakes Air at Mackinac County Airport
1220 N. State St., St. Ignace 49781, 906-643-7165
greatlakesair.net

Mackinac Island Airport
7700 Annex Rd., 906-847-3231
mackinacparks.com/more-info/mackinac-island-airport-2

• •

TIP

Great Lakes Air offers twenty-minute sightseeing tours over the Straits of Mackinac and Mackinac Bridge, by reservation.

SOLDIER ON
AT FORT MACKINAC

On a bluff 150 feet above the Straits of Mackinac, the whitewashed stone walls of Fort Mackinac contain fourteen buildings that date to 1780, when the British built the military outpost. The Americans and the British fought over the fort until it was returned to the United States after the War of 1812. Roam the barracks, officers' quarters, blockhouses, hospital, and bathhouse where, a post surgeon crowed, soldiers bathed "once a week, or more." Through videos, displays, and artifacts, the exhibit *Mackinac: An Island Famous in These Regions* sums up its history and evolution from a gathering place for Native Americans to a commercial center and tourist destination. Families head to the Kids' Quarters for hands-on activities; check schedules for tours, parade ground games and drills, and musket, rifle, and cannon firings by costumed interpreters.

7127 Huron Rd., 906-847-3328
mackinacparks.com

TIP
Your ticket to Fort Mackinac includes admission to the Richard and Jane Manoogian Mackinac Art Museum and the park's Historic Downtown buildings.

GET HIGH
AT FORT HOLMES

Big and shiny Fort Mackinac hogs the citadel spotlight, but there's a second stronghold at the island's highest point that's worth the uphill trek for its historic purpose and panoramic vista. During the War of 1812 the British constructed Fort George, a wood and earthen outpost positioned to defend the larger fort's vulnerable north side. When the Americans regained Mackinac in 1815, they renamed the redoubt after Major Andrew Holmes, a casualty of the previous year's Battle of Fort Mackinac. The abandoned fort was a popular tourist destination even as it crumbled, was rebuilt, and again fell into ruin. In honor of the bicentennial of the War of 1812, Fort Holmes was reconstructed from the original plans stashed in the National Archives.

2234 Fort Holmes Rd., 906-847-3328
mackinacparks.com

TIP
Admission and the miles-wide views are free. It's a great spot for picnics and stargazing too.

DRAW INSPIRATION
FROM MACKINAC ART

Built as the Indian Dormitory, this sturdy structure was snubbed by tribal members who came to the island to receive annual payments for the 15 million acres of northern Michigan land that they had sold to the United States in the 1836 Treaty of Washington. Problem was, the Indians preferred to camp along the shoreline. Their would-be housing was repurposed as offices, the schoolhouse, and finally the Richard and Jane Manoogian Mackinac Art Museum. Its eclectic collection of island-related and -inspired art includes centuries-old maps, paintings, intricate Indian beadwork, a vintage poster promoting the "island of romance," and Victorian souvenir glassware. Study the hand-tinted photographs by William H. Gardiner, who operated a local studio from 1896 to 1935, to see how much (and how little) the island has changed.

7070 Main St., 906-847-3328
mackinacparks.com

TIP
Take the family to the Kids' Art Studio on the ground floor to create a masterpiece as a memento of your visit.

CALL ON THE
GOVERNOR'S COTTAGE

The grand Victorian cottages that line the East and West bluffs above the town were built as summer retreats by the wealthy in the late nineteenth and early twentieth centuries. The fanciful homes feature architectural details such as turrets, wide porches, ornate woodwork, and stained glass. You can peek inside a fine example of one of the East Bluff cottages on Wednesday mornings, from June through August, on a free fifteen-minute tour of the first floor of the Governor's Summer Residence. Built in 1902 by Chicago attorney Lawrence Andrew Young, the three-story, eleven-bedroom shingle-style cottage is on the National Register of Historic Places and has been a perk of Michigan's chief executive's office since 1945.

Fort St. and Huron Rd., 906-847-3328
mackinacparks.com

TIP
For a close-up look at West Bluff cottages and panoramic Straits views, follow West Bluff Road to Pontiac Trail.

MARCH THROUGH HISTORY
ON MARKET STREET

The region's bounty of beaver, mink, fox, rabbit, and otter made Mackinac, and its Market Street, the fur industry hot spot from the 1600s until trade peaked in the 1830s. John Jacob Astor's lucrative American Fur Company was managed by Robert Stuart from his handsome, 1817 Federal-style home, now a city museum. At the American Fur Company Store, an accidental shooting in 1822 led to Dr. William Beaumont's pioneering study of the digestive system. When a gunshot to the gut of voyageur Alexis St. Martin created a wound that wouldn't heal, the doc gained a portal into the man's stomach for observation and experiments. The store and neighboring McGulpin House, Biddle House, and Benjamin Blacksmith Shop round out the Market Street sites that offer a look at early life on Mackinac.

Historic Downtown Mackinac
Market St., 906-847-3328
mackinacparks.com

Stuart House City Museum
7342 Market St., 906-847-8181
cityofmi.org/stuart-house-24

TIP

Admission to the state park's Historic Downtown sites (American Fur Company Store and Dr. Beaumont Museum, McGulpin House, Biddle House, and Benjamin Blacksmith Shop) is included with each ticket to Fort Mackinac.

HAIL THE
HORSE CULTURE

Since the automobile was banned in 1898, the island has reigned as the place where, as longtime Grand Hotel owner W. Stewart Woodfill declared, "Horse is king." Each spring about five hundred horses, specially trained to work in the unique island environment, return from their winter break at mainland farms, refreshed for another season of pulling carriages, taxis, and drays and getting saddled up for trail riders.

You can learn to ride in group or private lessons at the Mackinac Community Equestrian Center, where the nonprofit Mackinac Horsemen's Association preserves and protects local horse culture through classes, clinics, and horse shows. At Grand Hotel's working stable, visitors are welcome to inspect an impressive collection of antique carriages and sleighs and meet the resident royalty, a dozen Grand Hotel horses.

Mackinac Horsemen's Association
3800 British Landing Rd., 906-847-8034
mackinachorses.org

Grand Hotel Stable
Carriage Rd., 906-847-3331
grandhotel.com

Following a trail ride or carriage tour, hoof it to a horsey-themed eatery and soak up the equine atmosphere.

The Jockey Club
Riding hat light fixtures illuminate the cozy dining room with views of Grand Hotel's Jewel golf course.

1874 Cadotte Ave., 906-847-9212
grandhotel.com

Mustang Lounge
Hang at the Stang with locals. The bar and grill is named for both the popular Ford car and the horse tradition.

1485 Astor St., 906-847-9916
mustang-lounge.com

Pink Pony
The iconic hot pink mascot prances through the bar, dining room, and entertainment spot in the waterfront Chippewa Hotel.

7221 Main St., 800-241-3341
pinkponymackinac.com

Seabiscuit Café
The 1938 race horse phenomenon Seabiscuit inspired the decor and menu, which includes wine from California's Seabiscuit Ranch.

7337 Main St., 906-847-3611
seabiscuitcafe.com

GET THE SKINNY
ON ROUND ISLAND LIGHTHOUSE

The square Round Island Lighthouse not only marks the way for vessels passing through the Straits of Mackinac but also signals to ferry passengers that they're about to disembark at Mackinac Island. The light, with its fifty-three-foot red and white tower, was lit in 1896 and decommissioned in 1947. The condition of the abandoned structure deteriorated until local lighthouse lovers organized to raise funds and rescue the landmark. Over the decades, volunteers have restored the tower and outbuildings, and in 1996 the light came on again, using solar power. The small, uninhabited Round Island is a wilderness area of Hiawatha National Forest and is accessible only by private boat. The lighthouse, which is not open to the public, claimed its fifteen minutes of movie fame in the 1980 film *Somewhere in Time*.

Round Island Lighthouse Preservation Society
roundislandlightmichigan.com

PONDER THE PORTRAITS
OF NATIVE PEOPLE

They are Native American chiefs, warriors, princesses, and orators, captured on canvas to preserve the people and distinctive dress representing nineteen tribes. Commissioned by Thomas Loraine McKenney, superintendent of the Bureau of Indian Affairs, the portraits were painted between 1822 and 1838 by Charles Bird King while Indian dignitaries were in Washington, DC, to conduct business. The images, with biographies written by James Hall, were sold in bound editions as the *History of the Indian Tribes of North America*. The original paintings were destroyed in a fire at the Smithsonian in 1865, but lithographs of 120 subjects survived. Prints were donated to the Michilimackinac Historical Society, and copies of those make up the McKenney and Hall Portrait Collection that hangs in a circular gallery within Mackinac Island's Carousel Shops.

7463 Market St., 906-847-4011
michilimackinachistoricalsociety.com

TIP
The gallery sells prints of the portraits; locally made Native American crafts such as drums, spirit feathers, talking sticks, and jewelry; and books about local and regional Native American interests.

ADMIRE ART
SCULPTED BY NATURE

Mackinac Island's massive rock formations are the stuff of Native American legends, geological studies, and countless photographs, from hand-tinted Victorian-era prints to selfies. The natural wonders were created over millions of years from limestone that was broken and cemented together by ancient seas to form the hard substance recognized as Mackinac breccia. The breccia was shaped by churning waters that eroded softer materials and left towering stacks, sculpted shapes, and caves. Arch Rock, which reaches 146 feet above the eastern shoreline, is a favorite hiking and biking destination, a break for bicyclists circling the island (it's 207 steps up from the road), and a quick photo-op stop on narrated carriage tours. Boy Scout Gerald Ford, decades before he was president, posed for pictures on the natural bridge. Climbing the Arch is now banned.

906-847-3328
mackinacparks.com

TIP

Sugar Loaf, a dramatic breccia mass rising seventy-five feet above the ground, is the largest of Mackinac Island's many limestone stacks. View it from afar at Point Lookout, and then circle its base to comprehend its height. Other interesting geological features, marked on island maps, are Robinson's Folly, Skull Cave, Devil's Kitchen, and Cave of the Woods. If you must choose one, head to Crack-in-the-Island for a photo of you "stuck" in the split in the limestone.

APPRECIATE THE PAST
AT GRAND HOTEL

Built of mountains of white pine in a mere ninety-three days in 1887, the gleaming white Grand Hotel is one of the last remaining examples of America's Gilded Age summertime resorts. Catering to city dwellers who boarded steamships and trains to escape the heat and enjoy the clean, fresh air and water of Northern Michigan, Grand Hotel made Mackinac Island one of the country's premier leisure destinations. Under third-generation Musser family ownership and President Dan Musser III, the hotel is thoroughly modern in its accommodations, amenities, and wildly colorful decor, yet it maintains customs such as afternoon tea in the parlor, dressing for dinner, and evenings of dancing to a live orchestra. These are traditions to be savored and appreciated, perhaps from a rocking chair on the 660-foot-long porch, overlooking the glistening waters of the Straits of Mackinac.

286 Grand Ave., 906-847-3331
Reservations: 800-334-7263
grandhotel.com

TIP

No two of Grand Hotel's 393 guest rooms and suites, exuberantly decorated by Carleton Varney, are alike. Some have stunning lake views, while others are thematically designed, including seven First Lady Suites. You can sample the Mackinac summer cottage life for a night, week, or more at the Masco Cottage, a four-bedroom home that accommodates up to eight and includes Grand Hotel meals and amenities; the monthly rate is just under $90,000.

PAY YOUR RESPECTS
AT THE CEMETERIES

A great deal of island history rests in its three cemeteries, clustered along Garrison Road in the center of the island. Visitors are welcome to take a quiet and respectful walk through the Protestant Mackinac Island Cemetery, Ste. Anne Catholic Cemetery, and military US Post Cemetery. Although the civilian graveyards are historically named Protestant and Catholic, they are not strictly denominational. Originally, the burial plots were located near downtown churches, but, because of overcrowding, in 1850 graves were moved inland. The final resting places of Native Americans were disturbed by development over the centuries, but one burial mound is marked near the Ste. Anne Cemetery.

BRAKE
FOR ANISHNAABEK HISTORY

The stories and legends of the first people of the Great Lakes region, including the Straits of Mackinac, are told at six interpretive stations that dot M-185, the popular paved bicycle route that circles the island. Each panel along the Native American Cultural History Trail addresses an aspect of the Anishnaabek (Odawa, Ojibwa, and Potawatomi) and their connection to the island and the Great Lakes. Learn about their ceremonies and lifeways, the changes they encountered with the seventeenth-century arrival of Europeans, and the 1836 Treaty of Washington. The series ends with a look at the Anishnaabek in the twenty-first century. Each stop has benches and a parking area for bicycles. The project is a joint effort of the Little Traverse Bay Band of Odawa Indians and Mackinac State Historic Parks.

M-185, 906-847-3328
mackinacparks.com

GO TO
CHURCH

Ste. Anne Catholic Church offers a glimpse into the history of Christianity in the Straits of Mackinac, introduced by Jesuit missionaries in 1670. The original log church, relocated from the Lower Peninsula to the island in 1780, was replaced with the current graceful structure in 1875. Step inside to admire the artwork and stained glass; mass is offered year-round. On the lower level, the Images of Faith museum (open seasonally) contains baptismal, marriage, and death records dating to 1695, as well as art and artifacts from the church and parishioners. Also on Huron Street, Historic Mission Church is the oldest standing church building in Michigan. Now a museum, the island's first Protestant church was built in a simple, New England Colonial style in 1829–30.

Historic Mission Church
6670 Main St., 906-847-3328
mackinacparks.com

Ste. Anne Catholic Church
6836 Huron St., 906-847-3507
steanneschurch.org

TIP

Peek inside the replica of the seventeenth-century Missionary Bark Chapel in Marquette Park, near the South Sally Ramp to Fort Mackinac.

GREET THE DAY
AT MISSION POINT RESORT

The red-roofed compound that sprawls across eighteen acres of the sunrise side of Mackinac Island has a distinctively different vibe than its Victorian-era neighbors to the west. Mission Point Resort was built as a conference center by Moral Re-Armament, an international peace organization, in the 1950s and '60s and was gradually transformed into a hotel. Owners Dennert and Suzanne Ware are on a mission to improve the 241-room resort while respecting historical assets, such as the impressive, teepee-evoking lobby constructed with fifty-foot pine beam trusses, tons of natural stone, and twin fireplaces. Amenities at the full-service property include five dining options, free programs for kids, a full-service spa, pet-friendly accommodations, and activities such as staff-guided sunrise hikes. The Great Lawn linking the hotel and Lake Huron's shore is dotted with Adirondack chairs that invite a good read, freighter watching, or daydreaming.

1 Lake Shore Rd., 906-847-3000
Reservations: 800-833-7711, missionpoint.com

TIP
Climb the Mission Point observation tower for great views of the island, and on your way up take in the museum exhibits about Moral Re-Armament and the Straits of Mackinac and its maritime history.

FIRE THE CANNON
AT FORT MACKINAC

The *kaboom!* of cannon fire rings out from Fort Mackinac, thrilling visitors who gather at the upper gun platform to witness the ritual repeated by 1880s military interpreters several times throughout the day. You can don a blue kepi (a flat-topped army hat) and assist with the morning salute as the fort soldier positions, cleans, loads, and primes the artillery. And then, on the command "Ready, fire!" it's your job to pull the lanyard to trigger the first cannon volley of the day. No need to yell "Duck!" to the folks at Marquette Park and the harbor 150 feet below. The reproduction six-pound cannon fires a blank with three ounces of black powder. Anyone age thirteen or older can sign up in advance for the duty; the fee is fifty dollars and you keep the kepi (and earplugs).

7127 Huron Rd., 906-847-3328
mackinacparks.com

TIP
See the fort's only historic piece of artillery, the "Perry cannon," in the exhibit in the Soldiers' Barracks. The twelve-pound iron gun was with the American fleet that tried to recapture Fort Mackinac from the British during the War of 1812.

GO FORT
ON THE FOURTH

Celebrate Independence Day with an old-fashioned picnic and star-spangled festivities at Fort Mackinac, bedecked with the flags and bunting of an 1880s Fourth of July. Throughout the afternoon, visitors tour the fort and join in Victorian games and dances on the parade ground. That evening, the American Picnic spreads across the parade grounds, with patriotic music accompanying a feast prepared by Grand Hotel that includes BBQ ribs, grilled chicken, burgers, hot dogs, corn on the cob, watermelon, and more. (A separate ticket is required for the American Picnic.) The island's annual fireworks display caps the July Fourth celebration.

7127 Huron Rd., 906-847-3328
mackinacparks.com

TIP

Additional annual special events at
Fort Mackinac include a Vintage Base Ball
match-up between its team, the Never Sweats,
and a regional rival; Ghastly Mackinac, an
evening tour focusing on the grimmer aspects
of fort life; and Fire at Night, when the fort is
open at sunset for cannon and rifle firings.

DISCOVER A VIEW
NAMED ANNE

On the wooded bluff east of Fort Mackinac is a spot with a spectacular view of town, the harbor, and passing freighter traffic, with the curious name of Anne's Tablet. It's a memorial to Constance Fenimore Woolson, a nineteenth-century writer who, as a teen, summered on Mackinac Island and made it the setting of her first novel, *Anne* (available from the Island Bookstore). A successful but troubled writer, in 1894 Woolson died—possibly by suicide—in Italy, where she is buried. In 1916 her nephew Samuel Mather, a Cleveland industrialist and East Bluff resident, commissioned the tribute consisting of engraved benches and a large, bronze plaque that reads: "In Memoriam. Constance Fenimore Woolson—Author-Traveler—has expressed her love of this island and its beauty in the words of her heroine 'Anne.'"

TIP

Anne's Tablet is on visitor maps but is a bit of a challenge to reach. Small signs point the way on the wooded path along the bluff behind the fort and past the *Somewhere in Time* gazebo. Or, climb the Crow's Nest Trail stairway from the base of the bluff near the children's playscape at Marquette Park. Turn left when you reach Anne's Tablet Trail and wend your way to the overlook.

BEWARE OF THE
PUKWUDJININEES

At a place as rich in Native American lore as Mackinac Island, there are tales to explain everything from creation (the Great Turtle rising from the waters) to Arch Rock (a heartbroken Indian maiden's tears eroded the opening in the breccia formation) and Sugar Loaf (from a certain angle you can see the massive profile of an Indian brave who lives eternally in the seventy-five-foot towering rock). Then there are the Pukwudjininees, the mischievous little people of the woods of the Great Lakes region. According to a local guide, the playful fairies have been blamed for pranks such as removing or turning around directional signage on the trails and making maps disappear. As you hike or bike your way to island landmarks, be sure to pay close attention to your surroundings—and hold onto your map.

ENJOY A HISTORIC
NIGHT'S SLEEP

Because all of Mackinac Island is recognized as a National Historic Landmark, the majority of accommodations are in buildings with deep roots and fascinating stories behind their gingerbread trim and inviting, wicker-filled front porches. The Island House Hotel has been welcoming guests since 1852. Cloghaun Bed & Breakfast contains antiques original to the family who built the home in 1884. The sunny yellow, waterfront Bay View of Mackinac dates to 1891. Harbour View Inn is built around the home of Magdelaine LaFramboise, a successful fur trader and businesswoman in the early 1800s. There's not a chain property among the lodging options, which offer more than 1,500 rooms. Consult the Mackinac Island tourism office website for special packages, and an aid that helps select a place to stay based on type of lodging, budget, and location.

906-847-3783
mackinacisland.org

PITCH IN
ON A GRAND CLOSING

When Grand Hotel debuted on July 10, 1887, and for years to follow, the tourism season was just a couple of months long, and the structure was shuttered for most of the year. Gradually, the resort has been expanded and improved to accommodate guests for a longer period, from May through October. What happens during the six months when the lights are switched off and doors are locked? At the annual Close the Grand getaway, hotel historian Bob Tagatz presents a behind-the-scenes look at putting the resort to seasonal rest. While staff members bustle about, moving furniture and emptying the pantries and wine cellar, guests pitch in by carrying the one hundred rocking chairs from the porch inside for winter storage. The one-night, end-of-October package includes a casual buffet supper and continental breakfast. No fancy dress required.

286 Grand Ave., 906-847-3331
grandhotel.com

DO A GOOD DEED
AND SAY HI TO A SCOUT

From Memorial Day through Labor Day, uniform-clad Boy Scouts and Girl Scouts from across Michigan are stationed at Mackinac state park sites, ready to greet visitors, answer questions, and snap the occasional souvenir photo for folks. Each group of fifty to sixty scouts spends a week performing guide duties, flag ceremonies, and service projects, such as clearing trails and painting buildings. In 1929, Eagle Scout and future president Gerald Ford participated in the first Governor's Honor Guard. Now called Mackinac Island Scout Service Camp, the volunteer program was expanded in 1974 to include Girl Scouts. Troops bring their own food and supplies and bunk in the Scout Barracks near Fort Mackinac. They have free time to sightsee, hike, and ride bikes, but many say the best experience is meeting people from around the world.

SHOPPING AND FASHION

SOUVENIR SHOP
ON MAIN STREET

The most photographed and densely populated strip of Mackinac Island was first laid out by the British in 1781. Since the mid-1800s, when the island's tourism industry began, the road now known as Main Street has been the first impression for visitors disembarking from the ferries or arriving at the marina. Lined with picturesque, mostly Victorian-era structures, Main Street is a bustling cluster of dining, drinking, and lodging establishments; bicycle rentals; and shops. Lots of shops. The mix of merchandise ranges from fudge to novelty items, postcards, T-shirts, and sweatshirts (yes, Mackinac can be chilly even in summer) to fine art and jewelry. Somewhere in between there's the giggle-inducing "funusual" stuff of Caddywampus, a cheeky shop tucked under the Main Street Inn.

Caddywampus
498 Main St., 231-881-3972
facebook.com/caddywampusonmackinac

STROLL MARKET STREET'S
GALLERY ROW

Running parallel to Main Street, Market Street has served the same purpose since it was a center of commerce in the fur trade era, when John Jacob Astor built his American Fur Company there in 1817. Today, most merchants along Market Street deal in fine gifts and art, earning it the nickname "Gallery Row." Carriage tour drivers call it a fudge-free zone, so you won't find any free samples of the confection, but it's worth a stroll for the quality shops, including Mackinac's Little Gallery. Artist/owner Becki Barnwell, like most of the artists she features, specializes in scenes of the island. Maeve Croghan's "luminous nature paintings" reflect her time split between Michigan and California. She also carries jewelry and ceramic pieces by select artists at her gallery, Maeve's Arts.

Mackinac's Little Gallery
7410 Market St., 906-847-6400
mackinacslittlegallery.com

Maeve's Arts
7463 Market St., 906-847-3755
maevecroghan.com

BUY INTO HISTORY
AT DOUD'S MARKET

In 1884, Grover Cleveland was elected president, the Statue of Liberty was presented to the United States in France, and brothers Patrick and James Doud opened a grocery store near the Mackinac Island ferry docks. The Island House was welcoming travelers and blufftop cottages were being built, but Grand Hotel construction was three years away and fudgies were a thing of the future. Doud's Market, now located across from Marquette Park, continues to operate as one of the oldest family-owned grocery stores in the nation. The historic shop is completely current in its selection of fresh foods and produce, staples and specialty products, beverages, and prepared meals to go. Doud's Market and Deli, a popular spot for picnic fare and snacks, is located at the ferry docks amid the company's nineteenth-century roots.

Doud's Market
7200 Main St., 906-847-3444
doudsmarket.com

HANG IT UP
WITH AN ISLAND ORNAMENT

Round Island Lighthouse, Grand Hotel, the Little Stone Church, and Mackinac Bridge are some of the sites featured in the form of hanging ornaments handcrafted by local and regional artists for holiday display or year-round enjoyment. Browse around and you'll find an assortment of decorative and collectible mementos depicting local landmarks in a rustic sliver of wood or vintage-looking blown glass. For Island Breeze Fine Art Gallery, Michigan artist Merry Faith paints gold, red, and green bulbs in a colorful, folk art style. At Urvana's, delicately etched reproduction scrimshaw ornaments designed by Gary Kiracofe are elegant reminders of Mackinac attractions any time of year.

Island Breeze Fine Art Gallery
7395 Main St., 231-420-7423
islandbreezeofmackinac.com

Urvana's
7221 Main St., 906-847-3792
urvanas.com

JOIN THE
FUDGIE BRIGADE

In 1887, Sara Murdick's special candy recipes inspired her husband and son to open a Mackinac Island shop to tempt tourists with sweet souvenirs. Murdick's Fudge is still in business, one of several companies that sell so many thousands of pounds of the confection each day that visitors are called fudgies. Just try to resist the mouth-watering aromas that escape (aided by strategically placed shop fans) into the streets. Watch as candy makers stir copper kettles of secret combinations of sugar, cream, butter, chocolate, and flavorings. At just the right temperature, they pour the fudge onto marble-topped tables to cool while expertly shaping and paddling it into flat loaves to be sliced into half-pound slabs. Go ahead, have a free sample (or a dozen) and earn your fudgie stripes.

Grand Hotel, grandhotel.com

Joann's Fudge, joannsfudge.com

May's Candy, maysfudge.com

Murdick's Fudge, originalmurdicksfudge.com

Murray Hotel Fudge Company, mymurrayhotel.com

Ryba's Fudge, ryba.com

Sanders Candy, sanderscandy.com

TIP

Indulge in fudge-based foods, fudge cocktails, and family fun at the Mackinac Island Fudge Festival each August.

906-847-3783
mackinacisland.org

MAKE THEIR MACKINAC MEMORIES
YOUR OWN

The mother–daughter team of Jennifer and Natalia Wohletz had been making memories at their family's island summer home for many years when they put their artistic talents into their company, Mackinac Memories. Jennifer is a writer, custom book publisher, and photographer who captures close-up images of wildflowers, as well as wide views of the surrounding landscape. Daughter Natalia is a painter and printmaker whose linoleum block prints depict island scenes, from bicycles to horses and Victorian cottages. The duo interprets the sights, stories, and sentiments of Mackinac in images, books, coloring books, block prints, and note cards available through their website and at many Mackinac Island shops.

mackinacislandmemories.com

READ ALL ABOUT IT
AT THE ISLAND BOOKSTORE

The specialty at this independent shop is everything regional—fiction, nonfiction, and children's books, cookbooks, CDs, DVDs, calendars, and coloring books (for adults and kids) about Mackinac Island, the Straits of Mackinac, Mackinac Bridge, and the Great Lakes. But the Island Bookstore's shelves are also stocked with a well-rounded selection of children's and young adult books, bestsellers, and works from little-known presses. Shop co-owner Mary Jane Barnwell is a published author who appreciates local and Michigan writers, and she and her staff are well regarded for their recommendations and books bearing "staff pick" stickers. Located in the Lilac Tree Center. (There is a second Island Bookstore, also seasonal, in Mackinaw City.)

7372 Main St., 906-847-6202
islandbookstore.com

PLAY AROUND
AT GREAT TURTLE TOYS

Every inch of space in this colorful shop is jam-packed with playthings that support the Great Turtle Toys claim, "We're all fun and games." The joyful store carries an almost overwhelming variety and quantity of quality merchandise—most of it battery free—for indoor and outdoor activities, from crafts and puzzles to stuffed animals, rubber band slingshots, and board games. This is the place to buy one of the kites that soar over Windermere Point whenever weather permits. Known for its friendly and knowledgeable staff, the store has been a must-stop spot for kids of all ages since 1997. Located in the Lilac Tree Center.

7372 Main St., 906-847-6118
greatturtletoys.com

COMMEMORATE YOUR EIGHT
AT DESTINATION MACKINAC

You've seen the oval stickers bearing the numbers "26.2" and "13.1" for marathon and half-marathon runners. Jeri-Lynn Bailey thought that anyone who completes Mackinac Island's 8.2-mile perimeter route should have the same bragging rights, and she created not just a sticker honoring the accomplishment but a line of items and an entire store in which to sell them. The red Schwinn Hornet bicycle that hangs on a shop wall adorns Destination Mackinac 8.2 merchandise, from old-fashioned ringing bike bells to shirts and other wearables, mugs, water bottles, glassware, and magnets. Romantics will want the long and flowy scarves that come in soft colors and are meant to flutter in a cycling-induced breeze.

7221 Main St., 906-847-3430
facebook.com/DestinationMackinac

FLY THE FLAG
OF MACKINAC ISLAND

The banner representing Mackinac Island symbolizes key aspects of its culture and history in one pretty and packable souvenir. The flag's dominant blues and green represent the land and surrounding Straits of Mackinac. At the center, a graphic depicting the back of a turtle rising from the waters interprets the Native American legend of the origins of Mitchimakinak or Michilimackinac, Land of the Great Turtle. A horseshoe encircles the turtle shell, illustrating the importance of horses on the island. The three white stars have multiple meanings: the military influence; the flags of France, Great Britain, and the United States that have flown over the island; and the beauty of the night sky. You can find the banner for a traditional flagpole or garden stake at Flagship and Great Turtle Toys.

Flagship
1511 Astor St., 231-373-9962

Great Turtle Toys
7372 Main St., 906-847-6118
greatturtletoys.com

GET A TURTLE
TO GO
FROM THE GREAT TURTLE

Native American lore connects the turtle and Mackinac Island. To the Ojibwa people, the land resembled a turtle rising from the water, so they called it Mitchimakinak or Michilimackinac, Land of the Great Turtle. In a creation legend, the world is nothing but water until the great turtle Makinauk is called to lend his rounded shell to form the first land mass. Mackinac Island embraces the turtle and is home to the Blanding's, snapping, and painted (which is Michigan's official reptile) species. Remember your Mackinac visit with a turtle souvenir, such as *The Legend of Mackinac Island* from Island Bookstore, a whimsical "T is for Turtle" print found at Little Luxuries, ivory turtle jewelry from Urvana's, a turtle puppet from Great Turtle Toys, or of course, gooey turtle fudge from Murdick's.

mackinacisland.org

POP INTO POPPINS
AND WRITE HOME ABOUT IT

The art of the handwritten note is alive and well at Poppins, a happy place dedicated to lovely, handcrafted things that you didn't know you needed. Paper products star, from greeting cards and stationery to suitable-for-framing prints, decorative wrapping papers, and journals perfect for jotting down your impressions of Mackinac Island. Sharing shelf space with the writing materials, you'll find an assortment of candles, bath and body items, picture frames, small ceramics, and other decorative items that capture the fancy of owner Kate Nye. The British transplant's habit of carrying a large, catch-all tote—called the "Mary Poppins bag" by locals—inspired the name of the shop.

7388 Main St., 906-847-0334
poppinsonmackinac.com

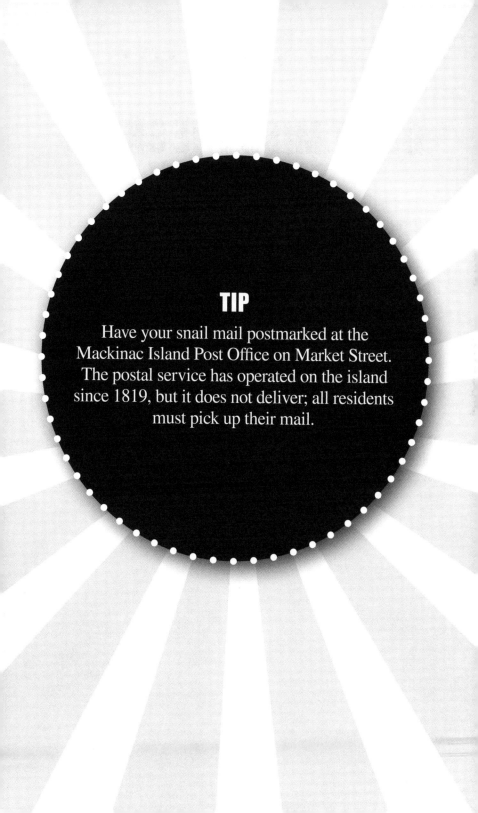

TIP

Have your snail mail postmarked at the
Mackinac Island Post Office on Market Street.
The postal service has operated on the island
since 1819, but it does not deliver; all residents
must pick up their mail.

DON'T MISS THE SHOPS
AT MISSION POINT

Take home the scent of lilacs in the luscious, heavenly scented Lilac Blossom body lotion and hand soaps from Lakeside Spa and Salon at Mission Point Resort. Shopping comes with views of Lake Huron at the resort's window-lined Marketplace, where The Boutique carries high-end resort wear and accessories, plus quality gifts and home accents. Step through the Garden Gate to adopt a cuddly, stuffed Nick dog, the black-and-white border collie charged with chasing Canada geese off Mission Point's Great Lawn. You'll also find casual clothing, retro toys and games, Mackinac Island books, and adorable, affordable ceramic bunnies and other curios in the cheery shop. Stock up on jars of the signature Mission Point marinara sauce and select wines (and a lemon bar for you) at Boxwood Coffeeshop & Café.

1 Lake Shore Rd., 906-847-3000
missionpoint.com

PLAN A GRAND
SHOPPING SPREE

Browse Grand Hotel's shopping concourse for fine clothing and accessories at Cagney's for men and the Colony Shop for women; bold Mackinac scenes at Oil Paintings by Marlee; baubles, including made-in-Detroit Shinola watches and Carleton Varney's Newbridge Silverware Collection at Grand Hotel & Co. Fine Jewelry; and toys for the kids at T. Richards. Grand Hotel devotees head to the Mackinac Market to stock up on the custom geranium body and hair products and collect colorful, blown-glass ornaments, including a Grand Hotel pot of its signature geraniums. This is the source for china with the house Camellia Rose pattern (an entire set or just the tea cup and saucer) and the six hundred dollars *Somewhere in Time* Grand Hotel music box—handmade, numbered, and signed.

286 Grand Ave., 906-847-3331
grandhotel.com

TIP
If you're not a Grand Hotel guest, you'll have to pay the ten-dollar visitor fee to access the shops.

GET YOUR HATTITUDE ON
AT THE ISLAND SHACK

In a corner of the little purple cottage on Astor Street, Janet Beeck quietly hand stitches fabulous fabrics into colorful witches' hats adorned with beads, spiders, ribbons, netting, feathers, and other trims. The fantastic head toppers deserve to be seen more often than just at Halloween (excepting, perhaps, the one that features a skeleton hand). Chock-full of funky yard art and seasonal decorations, Island Shack is the sister shop to Flagship, across the street. It specializes in "goods for gardens and breezes," such as wind socks, wind chimes, flags (including the official Mackinac Island banner), and more outdoor decor.

Flagship
1511 Astor St., 231-373-9962

Island Shack
1500 Astor St., 231-373-9962

FIND GIFT NIRVANA
AT URVANA'S

Urvana Morse managed the long-established Scrimshanders store for two decades before she bought the shop and expanded its merchandise beyond the delicately etched scrimshaw. She still carries scrimshaw items by Gary Kiracofe, the former owner, but you'll also find some antiques, plus paintings, Arts and Crafts-style pottery, pocket knives, folk art fish decoys, functional and decorative wooden pieces, and handmade tiles. Many of the fifty artists whose work she carries are from Michigan. The jewelry selection includes whimsical mermaid necklaces made of ancient mastodon ivory and sterling silver, and delicate dragonfly pendants of fossilized walrus ivory, pauna shell, and gold or sterling silver.

Urvana's
7221 Main St., 906-847-3792
urvanas.com

SPLURGE
ON LITTLE LUXURIES

Do you need it? Probably not. But you'll undoubtedly find something you'll want at Little Luxuries, a lovely shop that tempts with fragrant soaps and scented candles; decorative pillows and tea towels; kitchen accessories; and handbags, scarves, and jewelry. Expanding on the concept but featuring handcrafted items, owner Nicole Doud built on her success by opening The Artists Market of Mackinac Island. She stocks that store with the works of more than one hundred artists who create jewelry, watercolors, stationery, photographs, tiles, coasters, and one-of-a-kind frames and home accessories made of reclaimed wood. Watch for in-store artist demonstrations and appearances by makers of the goods that will suddenly seem essential.

Little Luxuries of Mackinac Island
7372-107 Main St., 906-847-9980
littleluxuriesofmackinac.com

The Artists Market of Mackinac Island
7344 Main St., 906-847-8225
facebook.com/artistsmarketofmackinac

NET A MEMENTO
AT A BUTTERFLY BOUTIQUE

Nature is the theme of the wide variety of items in the gift shops at the island's two butterfly attractions. At the Original Butterfly House, which also operates a second gift shop on Main Street, you'll find bright and bold paintings of the beautiful flying insects by local artist Noel Skiba, sterling silver jewelry featuring bits of butterfly wings, and complete butterflies preserved in acrylic boxes by John Jurek. Wings of Mackinac Butterfly Conservatory tempts kids—and parents—with a variety of books, educational toys, crafts, and science-related activities. Home decor and gift items ranging from prints to stained glass, colorful mobiles, and wearables fly off the shelves.

Original Butterfly House Gift Shop
6750 McGulpin St., 906-847-3972
originalbutterflyhouse.com

Wings of Mackinac Butterfly Conservatory Gift Shop
7528 Carriage Rd., 906-847-9464
wingsofmackinac.com

SNAP UP A SNARF
FROM SOMEWEAR ON MACKINAC

Wrap up your shopping with the snap scarf, or Snarf, an original and versatile accessory created by the local Sew UP Style Co. Designed and handmade by Julie Suggitt of St. Ignace, the Snarf is a long piece of fabric that you drape and tuck into place so it becomes—once you get the hang of it—a stylish neck wrap secured by large snaps. The Snarf comes in a variety of colors, prints, and fabrics for all seasons and is available at SomeWear on Mackinac, a boutique that also carries Michigan-made My Sisters Jewelry, plus footwear, clothing, purses, and accessories.

1547 Cadotte Ave., 906-847-3836
somewearonmackinac.com

GEAR UP
FOR UP NORTH

The image of Northern Michigan—known as "Up North" in the Great Lakes State—is a place of wild beauty, cozy cabins, campfires, deep woods, four-season silent sports, star-filled skies, and plaid clothing. Fulfill that vision at Canvas & Paddle, a new shop with a tasty selection of wearables, vintage-inspired home goods, and made-in-the-Upper-Peninsula Stormy Kromers (think Elmer Fudd flapped hats). Mackinac Outfitter has been selling sturdy outdoor clothing, backpacks, sleeping bags, and other gear on the island since 1982. The experienced staff wins raves for its knowledge of trusted brands Merrell, Patagonia, The North Face, Keen, and others. Swing by for a hammock and head to the woods of the inner island for a peaceful retreat.

Canvas & Paddle
102 Main St., 906-847-4020
canvasandpaddle.com

Mackinac Outfitter
7448 Main St., 906-847-6100
facebook.com/mackinacoutfitter

SUGGESTED
ITINERARIES

FUN FOR THE FAMILY

FOR THE TWO OF YOU

FREE FOR ALL

ACTIVE ADVENTURE

SPECIAL TO MACKINAC

WINTER ON THE ISLAND

INDEX